January 4

The essence of life is
not in the great victories and grand failures, but
in the simple joys.

Jonathan Lockwood Huie

....

....

....

....

....

January 5

Make a list

of ten people who helped you become
who you are today.

Thank half of them

before the sun goes down.

....

....

....

....

....

....

January 6

Get even! Help those who have helped you.

....

....

....

....

....

....

January 7

All the great things are simple,

and many can be expressed in a single word:

freedom, justice, honor, duty, mercy, hope.

WINSTON CHURCHILL

....

....

....

....

....

....

January 8

My lips will

Shout for joy

when I sing praise to you.

PSALM 71:23 NIV

....

....

....

....

....

....

January 9

Thank God for three things about winter.

....
....
....
....
....
....

January 10

Wrap up in a cozy blanket with a hot drink and
thank the Lord
for creature comforts!

....

....

....

....

....

....

January 11

Embracing an attitude of
gratitude is nourishing to the soul.

Steve Maraboli

....
....
....
....
....
....

January 12

Give thanks for
"all things"

for, as it has been well said,
"Our disappointments are but His appointments."

A. W. PINK

....
....
....
....
....
....

January 13

Choosing to
be positive
and having a grateful attitude is going to determine
how you're going to live your life.

JOEL OSTEEN

....

....

....

....

....

....

January 14

Start your day thanking God for the gift of it.

....
....
....
....
....
....

January 15

Whatever is
good and perfect comes
down to us
from God
our Father.

JAMES 1:17 NLT

....

....

....

....

....

....

January 16

Thank God for the freedom

to worship as we choose.

....

....

....

....

....

....

January 17

With joy without and joy within,

all is well.

JANET ERSKINE STUART

....
....
....
....
....
....

January 18

Those who look to Him for help will
be radiant with joy.

PSALM 34:5 NLT

....
....
....
....
....
....

January 19

Sometimes the simple things are more fun

and meaningful than all
the banquets in the world.

E. A. Bucchianeri

....
....
....
....
....
....

January 20

You will
go out in joy
and be led forth in peace.

ISAIAH 55:12 NIV

....
....
....
....
....
....

January 21

Life is a splendid gift

— there is nothing small about it.

FLORENCE NIGHTINGALE

....
....
....
....
....
....

January 22

Thank God
for His gifts.

Even if they aren't the ones you asked for.

....

....

....

....

....

....

January 23

Every morning seems to say:
There's something happy on the way.

HENRY VAN DYKE

....

....

....

....

....

....

January 24

Live for today but
hold your hands
open to tomorrow.

BARBARA JOHNSON

....

....

....

....

....

....

January 25

It's not what you do
but how much love
you put into it
that matters.

RICK WARREN

....
....
....
....
....
....

January 26

Be a support to new moms

who don't have a lot of family support—
especially single moms, military wives,
and moms in underemployed families.

....
....
....
....
....
....

January 27

Bring sunshine
into the life
of someone else

and you'll be warmed by it yourself.

....

....

....

....

....

....

January 28

Write
"I thank God for you"
on a sticky note and leave it
for someone who needs that reminder.

....
....
....
....
....
....

January 29

It's the simple things in life that are the most extraordinary.

PAULO COELHO

....

....

....

....

....

....

January 30

Instead of a curse,
offer a prayer
for the driver who seems lacking
in common sense.

....

....

....

....

....

....

January 31

Celebrate God all day,
every day.

I mean, *revel* in him!

PHILIPPIANS 4:4 MSG

....
....
....
....
....
....

February 1

Joy is the infallible sign of the presence of God.

Pierre Teilhard de Chardin

....
....
....
....
....
....

February 2

There is a time to

pour out your affections on one you love.

And when the time comes—seize it, don't miss it.

MAX LUCADO

....

....

....

....

....

....

February 3

Tell your best friend how much she/he means to you.

....

....

....

....

....

....

February 4

Take delight in the Lord,

and he will give you
the desires of your heart.

PSALM 37:4 NIV

....

....

....

....

....

....

February 5

Give your burden to the Lord,
and don't pick it up again.

Let Him dry your tears and give you back your joy.

JILL BRISCOE

....

....

....

....

....

....

February 6

Leave notes
of encouragement
in unexpected places.

....
....
....
....
....
....

February 7

Bless the Lord,
O my soul,

and forget not all His benefits.

Psalm 103:2 esv

....

....

....

....

....

....

February 8

It is always the simple that produces the marvelous.

Amelia Barr

....
....
....
....
....
....

February 9

Thank the Lord
for safety

on the road for you
and your loved ones

....

....

....

....

....

....

February 10

The spirit of gratitude is a powerful energizer.

WILFERD A. PETERSON

....

....

....

....

....

....

February 11

Do little things....

Little things can make a big difference for
someone who's not having a great day.

ELKE WALLACE

....
....
....
....
....
....

February 12

God has given each of you
a gift from his great variety
of spiritual gifts. Use them well to

serve one another.

1 PETER 4:10 NLT

....
....
....
....
....
....

February 13

Do all the good you can....

In all the ways you can. In all the places you can.
At all the times you can. To all the people you can.

JOHN WESLEY

....

....

....

....

....

....

February 14

Make your love visible

through little acts of kindness, shared activities,
words of praise and thanks,
and willingness to get along.

EDWARD E. FORD

....
....
....
....
....
....

February 15

Thank
your spouse
or significant other for
all he/she does for you.

....
....
....
....
....
....

February 16

No act of kindness,

no matter how small,

is ever wasted.

Anonymous

....

....

....

....

....

....

February 17

Cheer a stranger
with a smile today.

It's always nice to be acknowledged.

....

....

....

....

....

....

February 18

Joy
is the realest
reality,
the fullest life.

ANN VOSKAMP

....

....

....

....

....

....

February 19

Rejoice
in the gift
of the present.

....
....
....
....
....
....

February 20

A state of mind that
sees God
in everything
is evidence of growth in grace
and a thankful heart.

CHARLES FINNEY

....

....

....

....

....

....

February 21

Grow in the grace and knowledge of our Lord.

2 Peter 3:18 esv

....

....

....

....

....

....

February 22

Those who are happiest
are those who
do the most
for others.

BOOKER T. WASHINGTON

....

....

....

....

....

....

February 23

Make a simple dinner

for a shut-in or a family in crisis.
Include a note of encouragement.

....
....
....
....
....
....

February 24

Thank God no matter what happens.

1 Thessalonians 5:18 msg

....

....

....

....

....

....

February 25

Make sure to
give virtual and actual high-fives
to those who rock and rock hard.

SARAH WENDELL

....
....
....
....
....
....

February 26

Text or call your siblings and
compliment them on
their best qualities.

....

....

....

....

....

....

February 27

A cheerful heart is good medicine.

Proverbs 17:22 NIV

....

....

....

....

....

....

February 28

Gratitude is the ability to experience life as a gift.

It liberates us from the
prison of self-preoccupation.

JOHN ORTBERG

....

....

....

....

....

....

February 29

Leave quarters
on a gumball machine

for kids to find.

....
....
....
....
....
....

March 1

This is the day that the
Lord has made;

Let us rejoice

and be glad in it.

PSALM 118:24 ESV

....
....
....
....
....
....

March 2

**May your days be filled
with abundance, joy,
and gratitude to God,**
for all the gifts you have received
and have yet to receive!

LISA LADRIDO

....
....
....
....
....
....

March 3

**Buy coffee
for the next person
in line.**

....
....
....
....
....
....

March 4

Draw near to Me with a
grateful heart, and
My presence will fill you with joy and peace.

SARAH YOUNG

....
....
....
....
....
....

March 5

The greatest wisdom is in simplicity.

Love, respect, tolerance, sharing,
gratitude, forgiveness.

CARLOS BARRIOS

....

....

....

....

....

....

March 6

**Practice being
a good listener
today.**

....
....
....
....
....
....

March 7

The grand essentials of happiness are:

Something to do, something to love, and

something to hope for.

ALLAN K. CHALMERS

....

....

....

....

....

....

March 8

Extend grace
to someone

whose actions offend or annoy you.

....

....

....

....

....

....

March 9

Whatever you do

or say, do it as a representative of the Lord...

giving thanks...

to God the Father.

COLOSSIANS 3:17 NLT

....

....

....

....

....

....

March 10

**Tell someone today
how much
God loves them.**

....

....

....

....

....

....

March 11

Happiness is not a feeling,
it is a choice.

To be happy,
one must choose
to be happy.

JOYCE MEYER

....

....

....

....

....

....

March 12

Give your spouse
or best friend
a foot rub.

....
....
....
....
....
....

Give thanks to the Lord,

for he is good, for his
steadfast love endures forever.

Psalm 136:1 esv

....

....

....

....

....

....

March 14

To be grateful
is to recognize
the love of God

in everything He has given us—
and He has given us everything.

Thomas Merton

....

....

....

....

....

....

March 15

Share a little joy
by donating pasta, canned goods,
and toilet paper to a local food pantry.

....
....
....
....
....
....

March 16

Nothing you do in this life
will ever matter, unless

it is about loving God

and loving the people
He has made.

FRANCIS CHAN

....
....
....
....
....
....

March 17

**May your blessings
outnumber
The shamrocks that grow,**

And may trouble avoid you
Wherever you go.

IRISH BLESSING

....

....

....

....

....

....

March 18

May the righteous

be glad and rejoice before God;
may they

be happy and joyful.

PSALM 68:3 NIV

March 19

Little deeds of kindness,
little words of love, help to
make earth happy
like the heaven above.

JULIA FLETCHER CARNEY

....

....

....

....

....

....

March 20

Send a postcard

from your city or state to a friend or loved one

telling them you're praying for them.

....
....
....
....
....
....

March 21

The art of
being happy lies in
the power of extracting happiness from
common things.

HENRY WARD BEECHER

....

....

....

....

....

....

March 22

If it is possible, as far as it depends on you,
live at peace
with everyone.

ROMANS 12:18 NIV

....
....
....
....
....
....

March 23

Gratitude...
takes nothing
for granted,

is never unresponsive, is constantly awakening
to new wonder and to praise
of the goodness of God.

THOMAS MERTON

....

....

....

....

....

....

March 24

Come, let us sing for joy to the Lord;

let us shout aloud to the
Rock of our salvation.

PSALM 95:1 NIV

....
....
....
....
....
....

March 25

The only
really happy people
are those who have
learned how to

serve.

RICK WARREN

....

....

....

....

....

....

March 26

Find an excuse to

spend ten minutes
with elderly neighbors:

Ask their advice. Compliment their roses.
Pet their dogs.

....

....

....

....

....

....

March 27

Gratitude paints
little smiley faces on
everything it touches.

RICHELLE E. GOODRICH

....

....

....

....

....

....

March 28

The Lord
has done great things for us, and

we are filled
with joy.

Psalm 126:3 niv

....

....

....

....

....

....

March 29

Say "thanks"
to the people who keep
the world turning.

Busboys. Custodians. Bus drivers.
Ticket takers. Food servers. Mail carriers.

....

....

....

....

....

....

March 30

Be consistent in your dedication to showing
your gratitude to others.

Gratitude is a fuel,

a medicine, and spiritual
and emotional nourishment.

STEVE MARABOLI

....

....

....

....

....

....

March 31

Love extravagantly.

1 Corinthians 13:13 MSG

....
....
....
....
....
....

April 1

Stop by a
hospital or nursing home.
At the front desk ask,

"Is there anyone who could use a visitor today?"

....
....
....
....
....
....

April 2

Find things
to be grateful for.

It is easy. You're alive;
that's a good thing to start being
grateful for right away.

ALLAN G. HUNTER

....

....

....

....

....

....

April 3

Be truly glad.
There is wonderful joy ahead.

1 PETER 1:6 NLT

....
....
....
....
....
....

April 4

Be on the lookout today for God's treasures.

Thank Him for showing you
His love in the little things.

....

....

....

....

....

....

April 5

Gratitude is

the explicit effort to acknowledge that all I am
and have is given to me as a gift of love,

a gift to be
celebrated with joy.

Henri J. M. Nouwen

....

....

....

....

....

....

April 6

Anxiety weighs down the heart, but
a kind word
cheers it up.

PROVERBS 12:25 NIV

....

....

....

....

....

....

April 7

Forgive and give as if it were your last opportunity.

MAX LUCADO

....

....

....

....

....

....

April 8

Every day is a clean,
new page from God for us to

start again.

....

....

....

....

....

....

April 9

Brighten a rainy day

for someone by sharing your umbrella.

....

....

....

....

....

April 10

Take your place, take your chances,
take this moment to know....

You've got
something to offer.

HOLLEY GERTH

....
....
....
....
....
....

April 11

Each of you should
use whatever gift
you have
received to serve others.

1 Peter 4:10 NIV

....

....

....

....

....

....

April 12

God wants you to have a good life,

a life filled with love, joy,
peace, and fulfillment.

JOEL OSTEEN

....

....

....

....

....

....

April 13

Fix your thoughts on what is true,

and honorable, and right,
and pure, and lovely, and admirable.

PHILIPPIANS 4:8 NLT

....
....
....
....
....
....

April 14

Thank the Lord for the roof over your head,

be it ever so humble.

....

....

....

....

....

....

April 15

We can focus on all the things we don't like,
or we can begin to search for
the things we do like and

be grateful

for them.

ADAM HAMILTON

....

....

....

....

....

....

April 16

If you want to do the work of God,

pay attention
to people....

Especially the people nobody else notices.

JOHN ORTBERG

....

....

....

....

....

....

April 17

Personally deliver
a special treat

to someone
who doesn't get out much.

....

....

....

....

....

....

April 18

Generous hands
are blessed hands

because they give bread to the poor.

PROVERBS 22:9 MSG

....

....

....

....

....

....

April 19

Volunteer
to clean up

even if it isn't your responsibility.

....
....
....
....
....
....

April 20

People are often unreasonable
and self-centered.

Forgive them anyway.

MOTHER TERESA

....
....
....
....
....
....

April 21

Happiness is itself
a kind of gratitude.

JOSEPH WOOD KRUTCH

....

....

....

....

....

....

April 22

Let us seek
the grace of a
cheerful heart,

an even temper, sweetness, gentleness,
and brightness of mind.

JOHN HENRY NEWMAN

....

....

....

....

....

....

April 23

A cheerful heart brings a smile to your face.

PROVERBS 15:13 MSG

....

....

....

....

....

....

April 24

In normal life we hardly realize

how much more
we receive than we give,

and life cannot be rich
without such gratitude.

DIETRICH BONHOEFFER

....

....

....

....

....

....

April 25

Think of someone who has made
a big impact on your life.

Write a letter

saying, "Thank you for…."

....

....

....

....

....

....

April 26

Live in the moment.

....
....
....
....
....
....

April 27

When we determine to
dwell on the
good and excellent
things in life,
we will be so full of those things that they will
tend to swallow our problems.

RICHARD J. FOSTER

....
....
....
....
....
....

April 28

Make it as clear

as you can to all you meet

that you're on their side,

working with them and not against them.

PHILIPPIANS 4:5 MSG

....

....

....

....

....

....

April 29

Treat each person
who comes across your path
with respect,
valuing the gifts and talents
they bring to the table.

....
....
....
....
....
....

April 30

If we try hard to
bring happiness
to others,
we cannot stop it from coming to us also.

JOHN TEMPLETON

....

....

....

....

....

....

May 1

Celebrate May Day.

Leave a small
May basket or bouquet
on your neighbors' front porches.

....
....
....
....
....
....

May 2

God is in control,

and therefore in everything
I can give thanks.

KAY ARTHUR

....

....

....

....

....

....

May 3

Let all who seek God's help
be encouraged.

PSALM 69:32 NLT

....

....

....

....

....

....

May 4

Happiness is

in contentment, gratitude, and love. It is

a lifestyle,

not a location.

OGWO DAVID EMENIKE

....

....

....

....

....

....

May 5

Thank someone today

for a kindness done to you,
however small.

....
....
....
....
....
....

May 6

Take a few moments to indulge
in your favorite dessert, and

thank the Lord
for the simple joy
of sweets!

....

....

....

....

....

....

May 7

Keep a smile
on your face.

ROMANS 12:8 MSG

....

....

....

....

....

....

May 8

Call your mom

and say, "Thank you for raising me.
I know it wasn't always easy."

....

....

....

....

....

....

May 9

Joy is found
in self-abandonment.

ELISABETH ELLIOT

....
....
....
....
....
....

May 10

God is able to bless you abundantly,
so that in all things at all times,
having all that you need,
you will abound
in every good work.

2 Corinthians 9:8 niv

....

....

....

....

....

....

May 11

Recapture the power of imagination...
and find that

life can be full
of wonder,

mystery, beauty, and joy.

SIR HAROLD SPENCER JONES

....

....

....

....

....

....

May 12

Play a game
with a child,
savoring the fun and laughter.

....
....
....
....
....
....

May 13

God gives gifts and I give thanks and

I unwrap the gift given: joy.

ANN VOSKAMP

....
....
....
....
....
....

May 14

God is fair;
He will not forget
the work you did and
the love you showed
for Him by helping His people.

HEBREWS 6:10 NCV

....
....
....
....
....
....

May 15

The full
value of joy
is discovered when joy is
divided among friends.

....

....

....

....

....

....

May 16

Tell someone
why they
make a difference

in your life that no one else
could possibly make.

....

....

....

....

....

....

May 17

Give your place in line to a frazzled parent.

....

....

....

....

....

....

May 18

Let us consider how to

stir up one another to love

and good works.

Hebrews 10:24 esv

....

....

....

....

....

....

May 19

Joy...
comes from within.

It is a state of being.

BILLY GRAHAM

....
....
....
....
....
....

May 20

Let God deal with the evil things others do.

Keeping love
in your heart
will protect you.

....

....

....

....

....

....

May 21

Do not be overcome by evil, but

overcome evil
with good.

ROMANS 12:21 NIV

....

....

....

....

....

....

May 22

Every breath
we draw is a
gift of His love.

Thomas Merton

....

....

....

....

....

....

May 23

Instead of just saying,
"Great message,"

compliment the speaker
on specifics

that touched your mind and heart.

....

....

....

....

....

....

May 21

Make the most
of every opportunity.

COLOSSIANS 4:5 NIV

....
....
....
....
....
....

May 25

In a retail store or restaurant,
tell the manager when you
get exceptional service.

Good words trickle down

and are much appreciated.

....
....
....
....
....
....

May 26

Mail a thank-you card

or care package to a soldier.

....

....

....

....

....

....

May 27

When we are generous

—to God and to our families, friends, neighbors,
and others who are in need—

our hearts are filled with joy.

ADAM HAMILTON

....

....

....

....

....

....

May 28

Though they only take a second to say,

thank-yous
leave a warm feeling
behind

that can last for hours.

KENT ALLAN REES

....

....

....

....

....

....

May 29

Be joyful in hope,

patient in affliction,
faithful in prayer.

ROMANS 12:12 NIV

....
....
....
....
....
....

May 30

Give thanks to the Lord for this day

and all the good things
He has in store for you.

....
....
....
....
....
....

May 31

I will be glad
and rejoice

in you;
I will sing the praises of your name,
O Most High.

PSALM 9:2 NIV

....
....
....
....
....
....

June 1

When
your mind is occupied
with thanking God,
you have no time for worry or complaining.

SARAH YOUNG

....

....

....

....

....

....

June 2

It is only
with gratitude that
life becomes rich.

DIETRICH BONHOEFFER

....

....

....

....

....

....

June 3

I will be joyful in God.

HABAKKUK 3:18 NIV

....

....

....

....

....

....

June 4

Thank God for the times
He has shown you mercy
by not giving you what you want.

....
....
....
....
....
....

June 5

Do not forget
little kindnesses,

and do not remember
small faults.

CHINESE PROVERB

....

....

....

....

....

June 6

Do not withhold good
from those who deserve it when

it's in your power
to help them.

PROVERBS 3:27 NLT

....

....

....

....

....

....

June 7

One grateful thought is a ray of sunshine.

A hundred such thoughts paint a sunrise.
A thousand will rival
the glaring sky at noonday.

RICHELLE E. GOODRICH

....

....

....

....

....

....

June 8

Take your best friend
out for lunch or coffee and
**tell her the things
you appreciate
about her.**

....

....

....

....

....

....

June 9

If we fill our lives
with simple good things
and constantly thank God for them,

we will be joyful.

RICHARD J. FOSTER

....
....
....
....
....
....

June 10

A grateful perspective brings happiness

and abundance
into a person's life.

ANDY ANDREWS

....

....

....

....

....

....

June 11

Trust in the Lord
and do good.

PSALM 37:3 NIV

....
....
....
....
....
....

June 12

Make a batch of cookies for a friend

or neighbor who could use some cheer.

....

....

....

....

....

....

June 13

"Thank you"
is a wonderful phrase.
Use it. It will add stature to your soul.

MARJORIE PAY HINCKLEY

....
....
....
....
....
....

June 14

Take a moment to
really look
at your country's flag
and be thankful for all that it symbolizes.

....

....

....

....

....

....

June 15

It is
a wise person
who does not grieve for the things
which she has not, but
rejoices
for those which she has.

EPICTETUS

....

....

....

....

....

....

June 16

It is good for our hearts to be strengthened by grace.

HEBREWS 13:9 NIV

....

....

....

....

....

....

June 17

A mindset of
gratitude
lifts the veil of bitterness and
**allows you to see
beauty and possibility.**

STEVE MARABOLI

....

....

....

....

....

....

June 18

Get up early and
revel in the beauty of the sunrise.

....

....

....

....

....

....

June 19

We show our gratitude
by giving back

to God a part of that
which He has given to us.

BILLY GRAHAM

....

....

....

....

....

....

June 20

Enter into His gates
with thanksgiving,

and into His courts with praise.

PSALM 100:4 NKJV

....

....

....

....

....

....

June 21

Simplify your life

by letting go of unnecessary things.

....

....

....

....

....

....

June 22

If we have enough
food and clothing,
let us be content.

1 Timothy 6:8 NLT

....

....

....

....

....

....

June 23

The moment one gives
close attention to anything,

even a blade of grass,

it becomes a

mysterious, awesome, indescribably

magnificent world in itself.

HENRY MILLER

....

....

....

....

....

....

June 24

Take a moment today to
gaze on the wonder of God's creation.

....
....
....
....
....
....

June 25

Be thankful
for dirty dishes;

they remind us we have food to eat
and precious mouths to feed!

....
....
....
....
....
....

June 26

Love like there's no tomorrow,

and if tomorrow comes,
love again.

MAX LUCADO

....
....
....
....
....
....

June 27

You're far happier giving than getting.

ACTS 20:35 MSG

....

....

....

....

....

....

June 28

Hand out Popsicles
to the kids in your neighborhood
on a hot day.

....
....
....
....
....
....

June 29

Joy is the simplest form of gratitude.

KARL BARTH

....
....
....
....
....
....

June 30

You thrill me, Lord,

with all you have done for me!

PSALM 92:4 NLT

....
....
....
....
....
....

July 1

Thank a
police officer
for his hard work

in upholding the law
and keeping your community safe.

....

....

....

....

....

....

July 2

The best way to pay
for a lovely moment is to

enjoy it.

RICHARD BACH

....
....
....
....
....
....

July 3

I will sing to
the Lord,
because He
has dealt
bountifully with me.

PSALM 13:6 NASB

....

....

....

....

....

....

July 4

Freedom
did not come free....

Thank God we live in a country people are trying
to break into, and not a country
people are trying to break out of.

MIKE HUCKABEE

....

....

....

....

....

....

July 5

Reflect upon your present blessings,

of which every person has plenty;
not on your past misfortunes
of which all have some.

CHARLES DICKENS

....
....
....
....
....
....

July 6

What a stack of blessing you have piled up

for those who worship you.

PSALM 31:19 MSG

....

....

....

....

....

....

July 7

Welcome the
new neighbors

with flowers and brownies.
Or maybe meet the longtime
neighbors you've never talked with!

....

....

....

....

....

....

July 8

Live openly and expansively!

2 Corinthians 6:13 MSG

....
....
....
....
....
....

July 9

Whenever we are appreciative,
we are filled with a
sense of well-being
and swept up by the feeling of joy.

M. J. Ryan

....

....

....

....

....

....

July 10

On a hot day,
meet your mail carrier
at the mailbox
with an ice water to go
and offer a "thank you!"

....
....
....
....
....
....

July 11

Feeling grateful
or appreciative of someone
or something in your life
actually attracts
more of the things that you appreciate
and value into your life.

CHRISTIANE NORTHRUP

....

....

....

....

....

....

Give, and you will receive.

LUKE 6:38 NLT

....

....

....

....

....

....

July 13

Slip a twenty-dollar bill to someone

you know is having financial difficulty.

....

....

....

....

....

....

July 14

Enjoy the journey, enjoy every moment,
and quit worrying about winning and losing.

MATT BIONDI

....

....

....

....

....

....

July 15

Worship the Lord with gladness.

Come before him, singing with joy.

PSALM 100:2 NLT

....

....

....

....

....

....

July 16

Turn on some
praise music and
dance before the Lord!

....
....
....
....
....
....

July 17

In every circumstance that comes my way,
I can choose to respond in one of two ways:
I can whine or

I can worship!

NANCY LEIGH DEMOSS

....

....

....

....

....

....

July 18

The grateful person knows that God is good,

not by hearsay but by experience.

THOMAS MERTON

....

....

....

....

....

....

July 19

May all who seek you rejoice

and be glad in you.

PSALM 40:16 NIV

....

....

....

....

....

....

July 20

Cheer someone up

with a bouquet of flowers.

....

....

....

....

....

....

July 21

Seek to do good,
and you will find that

happiness will
run after you.

JAMES FREEMAN CLARKE

....
....
....
....
....
....

July 22

Offer to return
a shopping cart

to the store for someone
loading groceries into their car.

....

....

....

....

....

....

July 23

Go and enjoy choice food
and sweet drinks, and

send some to those who
have nothing prepared.

NEHEMIAH 8:10 NIV

....

....

....

....

....

....

July 24

Thank God
for all things

—hard days and lazy days, small moments
and large accomplishments, food to eat and hands
to wash the dishes.

....

....

....

....

....

....

July 25

A grateful heart recognizes that
all of life is a gift.

ADAM HAMILTON

....

....

....

....

....

....

July 26

I will be glad
and rejoice

in your unfailing love.

PSALM 31:7 NLT

....

....

....

....

....

....

July 27

Try to make someone laugh out loud.

....

....

....

....

....

....

July 28

We were filled with laughter,

and we sang for joy.

PSALM 126:2 NLT

....

....

....

....

....

....

July 29

Rejoice with those who rejoice;

mourn with those
who mourn.

ROMANS 12:15 NIV

....
....
....
....
....
....

July 30

Brighten a
weary mom's day

by offering to take
her kids to the park.

....
....
....
....
....
....

July 31

Gratitude
spurs us on

to prove ourselves worthy
of what others have done for us.

WILFERD A. PETERSON

....

....

....

....

....

....

August 1

Leave an extra
big tip.

....
....
....
....
....
....

August 2

In the endless
cycle of grace,
He gives us gifts
to serve the world.

ANN VOSKAMP

....

....

....

....

....

....

August 3

Do whatever will help you serve the Lord best.

1 Corinthians 7:35 nlt

....

....

....

....

....

....

August 1

Write a thank-you note to God.

....

....

....

....

....

....

August 5

Gratitude unlocks the fullness of life.

It turns what we have into enough,
and more.

MELODY BEATTIE

....

....

....

....

....

....

August 6

The best use of life is love.

The best expression of love is time.

The best time to love is now.

RICK WARREN

....

....

....

....

....

....

August 7

**Call or visit someone
who is sick or shut-in.**

....

....

....

....

....

....

August's

Focus on giving smiles away

and you will always discover
that your own smiles
will always be in great supply!

JOYCE MEYER

....

....

....

....

....

....

August 9

Gratitude is the
heart of contentment.

NEIL CLARK WARREN

....

....

....

....

....

....

August 10

God loves a cheerful giver.

2 Corinthians 9:7 NIV

....
....
....
....
....
....

August 11

Hug as many people as you can today.

....
....
....
....
....
....

August 12

This is the true joy of life, to
be used up for a purpose
recognized by yourself
as a mighty one.

GEORGE BERNARD SHAW, ADAPTED

....

....

....

....

....

....

August 13

Take a plate of cookies
to your fire station and
thank the firefighters
for their service.

....
....
....
....
....
....

August 14

Yesterday is dead,
tomorrow hasn't arrived yet.
I have just one day, today, and I'm going to be happy in it.

GROUCHO MARX

....

....

....

....

....

....

August 15

Every day we live
is a priceless gift of God,

loaded with possibilities.

DALE EVANS ROGERS

....
....
....
....
....
....

August 16

When anxiety was
great within me,
**your consolation
brought me joy.**

PSALM 94:19 NIV

....

....

....

....

....

....

August 17

Thank the Lord that

He has enough strength
to get you through this day,

even if you don't think you do!

....
....
....
....
....
....

August 18

Live one day at a time;
better yet,
make the most
of this moment.

JOEL OSTEEN

....

....

....

....

....

....

August 19

Be present
in the moment;
it is a gift of grace from God.

....

....

....

....

....

....

August 20

Satisfy us in the morning with your unfailing love,

that we may sing for joy
and be glad all our days.

PSALM 90:14 NIV

....

....

....

....

....

....

August 21

Cultivate the habit
of being grateful

for every good thing that comes to you,
and to give thanks continuously.

RALPH WALDO EMERSON

....

....

....

....

....

....

August 22

Let us not take what we eat for granted;
let us view our meals as an opportunity to
give our Lord praise.

DILLON BURROUGHS

....
....
....
....
....
....

August 23

Thank the Lord for the food
He abundantly
provides
for you
and your family.

....

....

....

....

....

....

August 24

Everything in life is most fundamentally a gift.

LEO O'DONOVAN

....

....

....

....

....

....

August 25

Gratitude brings JOY and laughter

into your life and into the lives
of all those around you.

EILEEN CADDY

....

....

....

....

....

....

August 26

Make a list of the good qualities in someone

who irritates you, and share it with that person.

....

....

....

....

....

....

August 27

Be completely
humble and gentle;

be patient, bearing with one another in love.

EPHESIANS 4:2 NIV

....

....

....

....

....

....

August 28

Two kinds of gratitude:

The sudden kind we feel for what we take;
the larger kind we feel for what we give.

EDWIN ARLINGTON ROBINSON

....

....

....

....

....

....

August 29

Thankfulness takes the sting out of adversity.

SARAH YOUNG

....

....

....

....

....

....

August 30

Praise someone for a job well done.

....
....
....
....
....
....

August 31

Sometimes
we do not realize
how much we have

to be grateful for
until it is threatened.

JOHN ORTBERG

....

....

....

....

....

....

September 1

Thank the Lord
for your job.

If you're a stay-at-home mom,
thank the Lord for the
privilege of being home with your kids.

....

....

....

....

....

....

September 2

To get joy, we must give it, and
to keep joy,
we must scatter it.

JOHN TEMPLETON

....

....

....

....

....

....

September 3

Clothe yourselves
with compassion,

kindness, humility, gentleness and patience.

COLOSSIANS 3:12 NIV

September 4

Be quick to say "I'm sorry"

when you've hurt or offended someone.

....

....

....

....

....

....

September 5

Clean out your closet, basement,
attic, or garage and
donate the good stuff.

....
....
....
....
....
....

September 6

If you concentrate on finding
what is good in every situation,
you will discover that your life will suddenly
be filled with gratitude.

RABBI HAROLD KUSHNER

....

....

....

....

....

....

September 7

Be kind and compassionate to one another.

Ephesians 4:32 niv

....

....

....

....

....

....

September 8

Take your coworkers a special treat.

September 9

Gratitude

doesn't change the scenery. It merely

washes clean the glass
you look through

so you can clearly see the colors.

RICHELLE E. GOODRICH

....

....

....

....

....

....

September 10

You make known to me the path of life;
you will fill me with joy in your presence,
with eternal pleasures at your right hand.

PSALM 16:11 NIV

....
....
....
....
....
....

September 11

You count on this—
the past ended one second ago.
From this point onward,

you can be...
used in many different
ways for His honor.

....
....
....
....
....
....

September 12

Gratitude can transform common days

into thanksgivings, turn routine jobs into joy, and
change ordinary opportunities into blessings.

WILLIAM ARTHUR WARD

....
....
....
....
....
....

September 13

When you arise in the morning, think of what
a precious privilege it is to be alive—to breathe,
to think, to enjoy, to love—then

make that day count!

STEVE MARABOLI

....
....
....
....
....
....

September 14

Always be eager to
practice hospitality.

ROMANS 12:13 NLT

....
....
....
....
....
....

September 15

Lighten up.
Humor is amazing medicine
for your soul.

....
....
....
....
....
....

September 16

How necessary it is to
cultivate a spirit of joy.

DOROTHY DAY

....

....

....

....

....

....

September 17

Let us be grateful to the people who make us happy.

MARCEL PROUST

....

....

....

....

....

....

September 18

Thank God!…

Tell everyone you meet what he has done!

Psalm 105:1 MSG

....

....

....

....

....

....

September 19

Sing God a song of praise.

He loves to hear you sing, no matter what you or others think of your voice!

....

....

....

....

....

....

September 20

The Lord...helps me,

and my heart is filled with joy.
I burst out in songs of thanksgiving.

PSALM 28:7 NLT

. . . .

. . . .

. . . .

. . . .

. . . .

. . . .

September 21

It is pleasing to God
whenever you
**rejoice or laugh from the
bottom of your heart.**

MARTIN LUTHER

....

....

....

....

....

....

September 22

**Don't be afraid
to laugh out loud.**

It makes people smile.

....
....
....
....
....
....

September 23

Thanks are the highest form of thought, and...

gratitude is happiness doubled by wonder.

G. K. CHESTERTON

....

....

....

....

....

....

September 24

Don't take a single day for granted.
Take delight in each light-filled hour.

ECCLESIASTES 11:7 MSG

....

....

....

....

....

....

September 25

Wherever you are, be all there.

Live to the hilt.

JIM ELLIOTT

....

....

....

....

....

....

September 26

Give thanks to the Lord,
for he is good;
his love endures forever.

1 CHRONICLES 16:34 NIV

September 27

Take a walk today and
thank God
for the sunshine
or mist on your face.

....
....
....
....
....
....

September 28

Let your good deeds shine

out for all to see, so that everyone
will praise your heavenly Father.

MATTHEW 5:16 NLT

....

....

....

....

....

....

September 29

**Do someone else's chore
without letting
anyone know.**

September 30

When we
choose
the pathway of worship and giving thanks…
there is a fragrance, a radiance,
that issues forth out of our lives
to bless the Lord
and others.

NANCY LEIGH DEMOSS

....

....

....

....

....

....

October 1

Gratitude
is an offering

precious in the sight of God.

A. W. Tozer

....
....
....
....
....
....

October 2

Always be thankful.

Colossians 3:15 NLT

....
....
....
....
....
....

October 3

Thank the Lord
for His protection

for you and your family.

....
....
....
....
....
....

October 4

Grace and gratitude
belong together
like heaven and earth.

KARL BARTH

....

....

....

....

....

....

October 5

Joy comes from knowing
God loves me.

DR. JAMES DOBSON

October 6

Joy does not
simply happen to us.
We have to choose joy
and keep choosing it every day.

HENRI J. M. NOUWEN

....

....

....

....

....

....

October 7

Renew an old friendship

by calling or writing someone you haven't seen
in a long time.

....

....

....

....

....

....

October 8

Bear with each other, and
forgive each other.

Colossians 3:13 ncv

....
....
....
....
....
....

October 9

Your life is a gift from God,

and it is a privilege to share it with others.

....
....
....
....
....
....

October 10

Gratitude and love
are always multiplied

when you give freely.

JIM FARGIANO

October 11

Stretch out your hand and
take the world's
wide gift of joy
and beauty.

CORINNE ROOSEVELT ROBINSON

....

....

....

....

....

....

October 12

Overflow with thankfulness.

COLOSSIANS 2:7 NLT

....

....

....

....

....

....

October 13

Do all things with a spirit of love.

....
....
....
....
....
....

October 14

We are his workmanship,

created...for good works.

....
....
....
....
....
....

October 15

We will harvest a good crop if we
don't give up.

GALATIANS 6:9 MSG

....
....
....
....
....
....

October 16

Offer to babysit

for a young couple
or single parent.

....
....
....
....
....
....

October 17

True happiness is
not attained through self-gratification,
but through fidelity to
a worthy purpose.

HELEN KELLER

....

....

....

....

....

....

October 18

You turned my wailing into dancing;
**you...clothed me
with joy.**

PSALM 30:11 NIV

....

....

....

....

....

....

October 19

Visit orphans
and widows

in their affliction.

JAMES 1:27 ESV

....

....

....

....

....

....

October 20

**Sponsor a
needy child.**

....

....

....

....

....

....

October 21

Let all that you do
be done in love.

1 Corinthians 16:14 esv

October 22

When God puts love and compassion
in your heart toward someone,

He's offering you
an opportunity
to make a difference

in that person's life.

JOEL OSTEEN

....

....

....

....

....

....

October 23

Say thank you to the fast-food counter person

before he/she says it to you.

....
....
....
....
....
....

October 24

When eating bamboo sprouts,
remember the man who planted them.

CHINESE PROVERB

....

....

....

....

....

....

October 25

Be delighted

at the prospect of a new day, a fresh try,
one more start, with perhaps a bit of magic
waiting somewhere behind the morning.

JOSEPH PRIESTLEY

....

....

....

....

....

....

October 26

Let all who take refuge in you be glad;

let them ever sing for joy.

PSALM 5:11 NIV

....

....

....

....

....

....

October 27

Give a care package to a homeless person.

....
....
....
....
....
....

October 28

May the Lord continually bless you.

Psalm 128:5 NLT

....
....
....
....
....
....

October 29

When God's people are in need,
be ready to
help them.

ROMANS 12:13 NLT

....

....

....

....

....

....

October 30

Give a loved one
a massage
after a long day.

....

....

....

....

....

....

October 31

Grace isn't a little prayer
you chant before receiving a meal.
It's a way to live.

JACQUELINE WINSPEAR

....
....
....
....
....
....

November 1

There is a calmness

to a life lived

in gratitude,

a quiet joy.

RALPH H. BLUM

....

....

....

....

....

....

November 2

One vote
can change a nation.
One life
can make a difference.
**That difference
starts with you.**

....

....

....

....

....

....

November 3

I sing for joy because of what you have done.

PSALM 92:4 NLT

....

....

....

....

....

....

November 4

Donate a shoebox full of goodies

to a needy child through
Operation Christmas Child
or other children's charity.

....

....

....

....

....

....

November 5

If you really fulfill the royal law
according to the Scripture,

"You shall love your neighbor as yourself,"

you are doing well.

JAMES 2:8 ESV

....

....

....

....

....

....

November 6

We are called to

a settled

happiness in the Lord

whose joy is our strength.

Amy Carmichael

....

....

....

....

....

....

November 7

Bring joy to a child

by helping him/her make a craft project.

....

....

....

....

....

....

November 8

As long as
thanks is possible, then

joy is always possible.

ANN VOSKAMP

....
....
....
....
....
....

November 9

Sing...to God with thankful hearts.

COLOSSIANS 3:16 NLT

....
....
....
....
....
....

November 10

Gratitude is a lifestyle.

NANCY LEIGH DEMOSS

....

....

....

....

....

....

November 11

Thank a soldier for their service to our country.

Offer to pay for their meal
if you have the opportunity.

....

....

....

....

....

....

November 12

Tell of his works
with songs of joy.

PSALM 107:22 NIV

....

....

....

....

....

....

November 13

The Lord's goodness surrounds us at every moment.

R. W. Barber

....

....

....

....

....

....

November 14

Bless a family in need
by inviting them over for a meal.

....
....
....
....
....
....

November 15

Joy is really a road sign pointing us to God.

C. S. Lewis

....
....
....
....
....
....

November 16

Nothing else in all
life is
such a maker of joy and cheer
as the privilege of
doing good.

J. R. Miller

....
....
....
....
....
....

November 17

Lend your favorite books

to someone you think would enjoy them.

....
....
....
....
....
....

November 18

**Gratitude changes the
pangs of memory
into a tranquil joy.**

DIETRICH BONHOEFFER

....

....

....

....

....

....

November 19

It is easy to
be thankful
for the good things. A life of rich fulfillment
comes to those who are also thankful
for the setbacks.

....
....
....
....
....
....

November 20

Be a child again.

Flirt. Giggle. Dip your cookies
in your milk. Take a nap.
Say you're sorry if you hurt someone.
Chase a butterfly.

MAX LUCADO

....

....

....

....

....

....

November 21

Around the meal table,
count all the things you have that money can't buy.

....
....
....
....
....
....

November 22

Gratitude is the real treasure

God wants us to find, because it isn't the pot of gold but the rainbow that colors our world.

RICHELLE E. GOODRICH

....

....

....

....

....

....

November 23

Rejoice! Celebrate all the good things

that God, your God, has given you
and your family.

DEUTERONOMY 26:10–11 MSG

....

....

....

....

....

....

November 24

God gave you a gift of 86,400 seconds today.

Have you used one to say "thank you"?

WILLIAM A. WARD

....

....

....

....

....

....

November 25

True gratitude,
like true love,
**is shown
through actions,**
not words.

....

....

....

....

....

....

November 26

Eat and drink and enjoy the fruits of [your] labor,

for these are gifts from God.

ECCLESIASTES 3:13 NLT

November 27

Make a list of the top ten things you are thankful for.

....

....

....

....

....

....

November 28

A cup of cold water is enough to put tears in the eyes of God.

God celebrates
our feeble expressions of gratitude.

Richard J. Foster

....

....

....

....

....

....

November 29

I have never met
a truly thankful,
appreciative person
who was not
profoundly happy.

NEIL CLARK WARREN

....

....

....

....

....

....

November 30

Deep, contented joy comes from a place of complete security

and confidence [in God].

CHARLES R. SWINDOLL

....

....

....

....

....

....

December 1

If we pray,
we will become
[the] sunshine of God's love
—in our own home, the place where we live,
and in the world at large.

MOTHER TERESA

....

....

....

....

....

....

December 2

Do not neglect to do good and to
share what you have.

HEBREWS 13:16 ESV

....

....

....

....

....

....

December 3

Donate a gift to the child
of a prison inmate.

....

....

....

....

....

....

December 4

Love never thinks in terms of "how little,"
but always in terms of "how much."

Love gives, love knows, love lasts.

JONI EARECKSON TADA

....

....

....

....

....

....

December 5

The King will answer them,
"Truly, I say to you,
as you did it to one
of the least of these my brothers,
you did it to me."

MATTHEW 25:40 ESV

....

....

....

....

....

....

December 6

You make a living by what you get,
but you make a life
by what you give.

WINSTON CHURCHILL

....

....

....

....

....

December 7

Drop a gift for an underprivileged child

in your local Toys for Tots
or other donation drop box.

....

....

....

....

....

....

December 8

Behold, I bring you
good news of great joy

which will be for all the people.

LUKE 2:10 NASB

....

....

....

....

....

....

December 9

Those who love
are borne on wings; they run, and
are filled with joy;
they are free and unrestricted.

THOMAS À KEMPIS

....
....
....
....
....
....

December 10

When we are generous with what we have,

we find that unexpected blessings flow back into our lives,

catching us by surprise.

ADAM HAMILTON

....

....

....

....

....

....

December 11

Christmas is love in action.

DALE EVANS ROGERS

. . . .

. . . .

. . . .

. . . .

. . . .

. . . .

December 12

Offer to wrap gifts for a busy parent.

....

....

....

....

....

....

December 13

Why not begin operating under the idea that
God has given us excess,
not so we could have more, but
so we could give more?

DAVID PLATT

....

....

....

....

....

....

December 14

When they saw the star,

they rejoiced exceedingly

with great joy.

MATTHEW 2:10 NASB

....
....
....
....
....
....

December 15

My idea of Christmas... is very simple: loving others.

Come to think of it, why do we have to wait for Christmas to do that?

BOB HOPE

....

....

....

....

....

....

December 16

We are better throughout the year
for having, in spirit,
become a child again at Christmas-time.

LAURA INGALLS WILDER

....

....

....

....

....

....

December 17

Christmas is doing
a little something extra
for someone.

CHARLES M. SCHULTZ

....
....
....
....
....
....

December 18

Blessed is the season

which engages the whole world
in a conspiracy of love.

HAMILTON WRIGHT MABIE

....
....
....
....
....
....

December 19

Christmas is

not as much about
opening our presents as

opening our hearts.

JANICE MAEDITERE

....

....

....

....

....

....

December 20

Christmas…is

a fervent wish that every cup may overflow with blessings

rich and eternal, and that
every path may lead to peace.

AGNES M. PAHRO

....

....

....

....

....

....

December 21

Glory to God

in the highest, and on earth peace,

good will toward men.

Luke 2:13–14 kjv

....
....
....
....
....
....

December 22

Christmas!

The very word

brings joy to our hearts.

JOAN WINMILL BROWN

....

....

....

....

....

....

December 23

If we keep telling the Christmas story,
singing the Christmas songs,
and living the Christmas spirit,

we can bring joy and happiness and peace to this world.

NORMAN VINCENT PEALE

....

....

....

....

....

....

December 24

To us a child is born,

to us a son is given,

and the government will be on his shoulders.

Isaiah 9:6 NIV

....

....

....

....

....

....

December 25

For somehow, not only at Christmas,
but all the long year through,

the joy that you
give to others
is the joy that comes
back to you.

JOHN GREENLEAF WHITTIER

....

....

....

....

....

....

December 26

Celebrate Boxing Day today.

Deliver small gifts to the people who serve you all year,

such as your hair dresser, mail carrier, and bank teller.

....

....

....

....

....

....

December 27

Shovel the snow off of a neighbor's walkway.

....
....
....
....
....
....

December 28

Celebrate God.

Sing together—everyone!
All you honest hearts, raise the roof!

PSALM 32:11 MSG

December 29

Joy is the touch of God's finger.

PETER KREEFT

....
....
....
....
....
....

December 30

You crown the year with Your goodness, and

Your paths
drip with abundance.

PSALM 65:11 NKJV

....

....

....

....

....

....

December 31

Take advantage of His faithfulness and
make every day
a fresh start.

DEBBIE CARROCCIO

....

....

....

....

....

....

Ellie Claire® Gift & Paper Corp.
Brentwood, TN 37027
EllieClaire.com
A Worthy Publishing Company

The Simple Joys of Life: A Thought-a-Day Grace and Gratitude Journal
© 2013 by Ellie Claire Gift & Paper Corp.
ISBN 978-1-60936-811-1

Scripture quotations are taken from the following sources: The Holy Bible, King James Version (KJV). The Holy Bible, New International Version®, NIV®. Copyright © 1973, 1978, 1984, 2011 by Biblica, Inc.™ Used by permission of Zondervan. All rights reserved worldwide. The Holy Bible, New King James Version (NKJV). Copyright © 1982 by Thomas Nelson, Inc. Used by permission. The Holy Bible, English Standard Version® (ESV), The New American Standard Bible® (NASB), copyright © 1960, 1962, 1963, 1968, 1971, 1972, 1973, 1975, 1977, 1995 by The Lockman Foundation. Used by permission. copyright © 2001 by Crossway Bibles, a publishing ministry of Good News Publishers. Used by permission. The Holy Bible, New Living Translation (NLT), copyright 1996, 2004, 2007 by Tyndale House Foundation. Used by permission of Tyndale House Publishers, Inc., Carol Stream, Illinois 60188. *The Message* (MSG). Copyright © 1993, 1994, 1995, 1996, 2000, 2001, 2002 by Eugene Peterson. Used by permission of NavPress, Colorado Springs, CO. The New Century Version® (NCV). Copyright © 1987, 1988, 1991, 2005 by Thomas Nelson, Inc. Used by permission. All rights reserved.

Excluding Scripture verses and deity pronouns, in some quotations references to men and masculine pronouns have been replaced with gender-neutral or feminine references. Additionally, in some quotations we have carefully updated verb forms and wording that may distract modern readers.

Stock or custom editions of Ellie Claire titles may be purchased in bulk for educational, business, ministry, fundraising, or sales promotional use.
For information, please e-mail info@EllieClaire.com

Illustrations by Julie Sawyer Phillips
Compiled by Jill Jones
Cover and interior design by Jeff Jansen | aestheticsoup.net
Typesetting by James Baker

Printed in China
123456789-181716151413